How To
SHARPEN
Your LISTENING-TO-GOD Skills

How To SHARPEN Your LISTENING-TO-GOD Skills

Fred Parks Morris

WinePress Publishing
MUKILTEO, WA 98275

How to Sharpen Your Listening-to-God Skills
Copyright © 1998 by Fred Parks Morris

Published by:
WinePress Publishing
PO Box 1406
Mukilteo, WA 98275

All rights reserved. No part of this publication may be reproduced, stored in a retrieval system or transmitted in any way by any means, electronic, mechanical, photocopy, recording or otherwise, without the prior permission of the publisher, except as provided by USA copyright law.

Unless otherwise noted, Scripture quotations in this book are taken from the Holy Bible, New International Version, Copyright © 1973, 1978, 1984 by the International Bible Society. Used by permission of Zondervan Publishing House. The "NIV" and "New International Version" trademarks are registered in the United States Patent and Trademark Office by International Bible Society.

Printed in the United States of America

ISBN 1-57921-051-1
Library of Congress Catalog Card Number: 97-61560

ACKNOWLEDGEMENTS

On a summer day in South Carolina in 1975, I was speaking to the Easley Civitan Club on a pro-American business motivational subject. The program chairman stood up after my presentation, thanked me, and then said, "Mr. Morris, if you're so smart, why ain't you rich?"

The crowd laughed. I didn't. I was 27 and just beginning as an entrepreneur. I went home, canceled two remaining speaking engagements, rolled up my sleeves, and went to work. I never spoke again to a large group until June of 1994.

In those 19 years I built a company earning a profit of $250,000 a year while spiritually bankrupting myself. In May of 1987, I turned my business over to Jesus Christ. I watched Him whittle it down; and then I watched Him rebuild it. Then I watched Him carve out time for me to begin the ministry of Skyhook.

During my darkest days, Harold, my trusted friend and warehouse manager, gave me strength through his testimony, to carry on. In 1994, he invited me to speak to the men's breakfast of his church, Fountain of Life Pentecostal Holiness, in Piedmont, South Carolina.

Ray Buchanan, pastor of Fountain of Life, then invited me back to speak to the congregation for two Sundays. After those two days the fire never left my belly.

Acknowledgements

The Lord opened doors for me to study, grow, and teach. He pushed me when it was time to get with it. He stopped me when it was time to wait. I asked Him many times when I was to leave my chemical company and be in my ministry full time. One day a voice in the back of my head asked, "Where do you think you get your material?"

I began teaching Sunday school on a regular basis at my home church, First Presbyterian, in Greenville, South Carolina, in 1996. I was teaching a Sunday school for several weeks when a lively lady, distinguished in years, and eloquent of voice, sat in with a friend. She demonstrated an interest in my subject matter, and my presentation, and began to attend regularly whenever I taught.

A friendship developed and through our conversation I learned of her professional skills as a writer. When the time was right, I asked Evelyn Waldrop to be my writing coach.

I think she took the job more out of curiosity than anything else. But after several weeks I began leaving her study with the feeling I had been beaten over the head with a baseball bat. Then I knew she was in it for the long haul. May the lumps she raised never leave.

Almost five years ago, I was a helper at a dance club. The Shag, the official dance of the State of South Carolina, was the specialty. I was single then, and I made it a policy of never dating my dance partners. But this lady knew how to follow a lead. Well, the Lord was leading me. Now I was leading her, and she knew how to follow. It stuck. She also knew how to do something I had not found in a woman. That was to support me. That Sara has done from the day we were married. Her love, companionship, and portable sounding board has made me a very grateful man.

There are two places Sara and I go when we need a rest. The first is my family's old home place on the Chestatee

River in North Georgia. The second is my mother and dad's condo at Ft. Myers Beach, Florida. Mother and dad have always believed that it was essential to oil the gears with some "R & R" if you hope to work at your greatest potential.

I can make it to the old home place in a little over two hours. I'm in North Georgia quite often. I do fun work there. Stuff like chopping, sawing, painting, hammering, and cutting grass clears my head.

When I go to Florida, a twelve hour drive, I'm normally burnt out. I do nothing except sleep, walk the beach, raid the fridge, go out to dinner, and occasionally wet a hook.

Mother and dad have always seen to it that the lights were on, the furnace worked, there was a warm bed, and a place to get fed. This was true whether Sara and I were alone, with them in North Georgia, or with them in Florida.

My deepest thanks to my wife, Sara; to Evelyn, Ray, and Harold. My thanks to my mother and dad.

My thanks to First Presbyterian Church for the opportunity to teach the practical application of God's word.

To my Father in heaven, I humbly offer thanksgiving beyond words for the opportunity to glorify Him through the renewed success of my company, ADI, and my ministry, Skyhook.

CONTENTS

Introduction 11
Part One
Can We Really Communicate with God? 19
    It's Our Fault
    We Don't Listen
    We Don't Talk
    Communication with God Is Natural
    The Steps of Communicating with God
    David's Trust in God
    David's Communication with God

Part Two
Learning How to Communicate with God 43
    The Journal
    But What Do I Say?
    Some Tips and Suggestions
    How to Get God Really Excited about Your Life
    Examples from My Journal
    The Legacy of Your Record
    A Gentle Reminder

Part Three
Skyhook Ministry 63
    Statement of Faith
    About the Founder
    Current Speaking Topics

Part Four
Your Beginning Pages of Your
Communication Journal 71

INTRODUCTION

Many times when people achieve success, they forget that their success was the work of God. Such was the case for Fred Morris. Even though Fred forgot God, God didn't forget him. This is the story of the split and reunion of Fred Morris and Jesus Christ and the resulting tearing down and rebuilding of a little company in South Carolina.

The offspring of an entrepreneurial family, Fred Morris should have been more interested in building an empire than building a relationship with Christ. But Fred felt that a startup business could use someone like Christ on the Board of Directors. What better way could a company demonstrate Christian ethics, integrity, and a good reputation? So in 1976, Fred began ADI, American Distributing Industries, from the ruins of a door-to-door cleaning chemical company. He decided to bring Jesus Christ on board in an advisory position.

For the first few years, Morris and Christ worked very well together and tried some innovative ideas that were unheard of in business in the 70s.

The first was total honesty. Morris determined to be totally honest in recruiting his associates. He motivated them by sharing the financial information of his company. He was also totally honest about his products. Cleaning chemicals were 90 percent water. So why not admit it and charge a fair price, not what the market would bear, and pass the savings on to the client?

Introduction

The honesty filtered down through the company. The result was greater teamwork, sharing of responsibility by the employees, and a greater respect of what it took to run a company.

The second area of agreement was recycling. It was an industry-wide custom to throw containers away. It takes 100 years for plastic to decompose. To hire someone to wash drums instead of buying plastic to be thrown away was a no-brainer. So ADI began to leave large storage drums at clients' locations, never throwing them away. Smaller drums were washed and reused. This made ADI's packaging cost the lowest in the industry.

ADI also recycled its waste water. Instead of draining the cleaning water into the septic tank, they collected it in pools and let sunlight and the elements break down the waste and purify the water. They would use the water again to wash more drums and make more cleaning detergents. This was a decade before it was fashionable to recycle!

ADI grew explosively, acquiring cleaning contracts with national chains in less than three years. Then Fred became more impressed with his own importance. He argued more with his board member, Christ, and listened to Him less. Fred's own physical and material desires became more important. Fast money had come to him, so he thought he was gifted in making fast money in other places. So the stock and commodities market became a second home. Along with fast money came a fast lifestyle and associations with fast-lane people. The idealism that started his company was no longer there.

At age 39, Fred was earning nearly $100,000 per year; ADI was making an annual profit of $250,000. Fred was a writer, a successful speaker, a motivator, a human relations specialist, and a successful CEO.

But instead of being happy and satisfied, he was bored stiff. His life wasn't exciting or rewarding enough. In reality his life was coming apart. Fred didn't see the gradual erosion taking place. The fast lifestyle had become an addiction to intimate female relationships, alcohol, and gambling in the stock market.

One Sunday, at a church Fred was attending, one of the members announced that Mike Warnke, a Christian comedian, was coming to Greenville Memorial Auditorium. The member handed Fred a small paperback entitled *The Satan Seller*, Warnke's personal story. Fred had never read this kind of book. He was fast becoming a millionaire and thought he didn't need this kind of book. But he left the book in his truck.

One day, with time to kill, Fred picked the book up, scanned the pages, then began to read about Mike Warnke's wild, fast-lane life. Gradually he began to change his whole decision-making process.

Fred had trouble with the whole idea of surrendering. He had built his company. He had paid a price. He was president. Jesus Christ was on the board. They were a team. Fred called all the shots and had the final say. But that wasn't working. Every part of his life was empty. Nothing was rewarding any more. Both ends of his candle were aflame and fast approaching the center.

On a lonely road somewhere between Charleston, South Carolina. and Augusta, Georgia in the first week of May 1987, Fred promoted Jesus Christ from a mere member to Chairman of the Board of American Distributing Industries, Inc., and gave Him 100 percent of the shares of stock in the company. Christ took the position. There were a lot of things He liked and a lot of things He didn't like about the company.

Introduction

The next four years demonstrated God's awesome power at work.

Fred joined AA and quit drinking January 6, 1988. Breaking off several devastating amorous relationships created great pain and broke his heart. Then God's love began to fill the holes and cement the pieces of his life together. He had never realized such love and peace before. It was a love and peace he desperately needed to balance his life. "You build a relationship with God before you build a relationship with people," he said.

Then on September 27, 1989, Hurricane Hugo destroyed one half of Fred's company. "I watched 14 years of work be destroyed in 14 hours," he recalls. The recession of '90 and '91 took one half of what was left. Then the Gulf War plummeted the stock market, taking Fred's last remaining cash. God literally broke Fred and ADI down to the foundation and then began rebuilding from what was left. Here, in Fred's own words, is what happened.

> In January 1991, we were financially bankrupt, but I refused to declare bankruptcy. Our backs were against the wall. I made a pledge to tithe the increase of any blessing that came to me or ADI. But this was a different pledge. I pledged any increase, right down to crushed soda cans I found on the street.
>
> I picked up cans, but not to cash them in. The cans were a reminder of the biggest expense I had eliminated from myself and ADI..... my ego. My ego was in the way of listening to God. I looked at any blessing, no matter how small, as a gift from God. I wanted to be totally tuned in to any message that God was sending to me. I used picking up cans as a humility exercise.
>
> I had no idea how much power there was in what I was doing. I never knew how excited God could get

about someone trying to listen better to what He was saying.

He creates the situations that allow us to see and remove our limitations. He invests in us and knows our greatest weaknesses and potentials. He knows the path we are supposed to take to achieve our greatest growth. He also knows the pitfalls along the way. This is an incredible fact to comprehend.

I also started a diary, a record of my talking and listening to God. I recorded every blessing of any kind that God bestowed on me, whether it was strange coincidences, money out of the blue, new clients coming from nowhere. I recorded guidance to new ideas, or people, steering me away from bad situations. This went for every part of my business, family, or personal life. When I could, I put a money value on the blessings that came to me. I then tithed from that value.

For every dollar, God could just as easily have given me 90 cents. But He gave me a whole dollar. He gave me a bunch of them. The least I could do was give Him back 10 cents of each dollar. I began to get a genuine appreciation for His power. I learned what a deep joy it is to give. I also learned how excited He could become when I managed His money properly.

I also wrote to God in my record. I asked Him my toughest, deepest questions about my life. The more questions I asked, the more questions I had to ask. I never realized how many things I was trying to do without any help. I never realized how many forks in the road I faced. It's different when it's on paper. It's more concrete. You sink your teeth into the questions more. I thanked Him in the record, too. Recording my thanks meant more. He knew it and I knew it.

Weird stuff began to happen. Old clients came back. New clients came out of the blue. My company slowly began to rebuild without any push from me. I just fol-

Introduction

lowed the direction that God set out for me. I listened to my hunches more and calculated less. Most of the hunches were base hits. Some of the hunches were even home runs!

Demands for bills to be paid suddenly stopped. People I owed stopped bugging me, for some reason. As my company grew, I gradually began to pay the old bills. Even the tax people forgot me. That's right, forgot me! One tax collector told me that my file had just vanished from the screen! Mysteriously they didn't remember me until I had enough cash flow to pay them.

My personal life was organized by a phantom Social Director. People who wasted my time were removed from my life. Instead, time was easily created for people I did need to see. The time I never thought I had to go to church was created. Then the whole Sunday, with very few exceptions, was carved out. If I needed a rest, the day was arranged for me without my help. If there were family emergencies, time was arranged for me to be away. There were no company emergencies when there were family emergencies.

I quit worrying. I had freedom. I had peace. The Chairman of the Board came through with His promises: ask Him questions, listen to His answers, do what He wants you to do the way He wants you to do it. Thank Him, praise Him, honor Him with your first fruits. You will receive freedom, peace, and more blessings than you can handle.

ADI is currently a profitable company in Simpsonville, South Carolina. Fred Morris is founder of Skyhook, a ministry involved in teaching how to build a productive relationship with God through finding your talents, stewardship, and improving your listening-to-God skills.

(Jeremiah 11:6–10)

The Lord said to me, "Proclaim all these words in the towns of Judah and in the streets of Jerusalem: 'Listen to the terms of this covenant and follow them. From the time I brought your forefathers up from Egypt until today, I warned them again and again, saying "Obey me." But they did not listen or pay attention; instead, they followed the stubbornness of their evil hearts. So I brought on them all the curses of the covenant I had commanded them to follow but that they did not keep.'"

Then the Lord said to me, "There is a conspiracy among the people of Judah and those who live in Jerusalem. They have returned to the sins of their forefathers, who refused to listen to my words. They have followed other Gods to serve them."

PART ONE

CAN WE REALLY COMMUNICATE WITH GOD?

It's Our Fault

Relationships. What would we do without them? They make the grass greener, the sky bluer, and the clouds whiter. Relationships are teams on Saturday afternoons. They are teams Monday through Friday. They move mountains. They build skyscrapers. They are the reason we are not in constant war. They are our protection that gives us peace.

We live in an interdependent society. The complexities of interlocking societies make independent living impossible. Without relationships, the country, the state, and the town we call home would be virtually nonexistent.

Suppose you meet someone through working or socializing and you would like to build a relationship with that person. It may be a friendship, a work team, or something deeper. How do you go about it?

You begin to share information, small talk at first, to see if you have some common ground. You might spend time with that person to see how well you do things together. You will want to discover if you can trust that person with information. Then, when critical situations arise, you will learn if you can count on that person to be there when times are tough and you really need a friend.

Relationships require communication in order to grow. Take away the communication and the relationship becomes strained, gets off track, and eventually dies.

Communication in a relationship requires not only a desire to talk and listen with love and respect, but a desire to talk and listen in the manner that is rewarding to the relationship. If there is no love and respect in the communication, the relationship doesn't grow. It is torn down instead of built up.[1]

We put a great deal of time and effort into building relationships. Why do we think it is any different when it comes to building a relationship with Jesus Christ? Building a relationship with Jesus Christ encounters the same problems as building a relationship with anyone: We take Him for granted. We don't lovingly talk to Him enough. We respectfully listen to Him only as a last resort.

We Don't Listen

It is widely felt that God only speaks to us in the way a conductor would lead his orchestra in the William Tell Overture...by blowing us out of the saddle! That's because we tend to look only at the Oscar-winning examples: Moses and the burning bush; Paul blinded on the Damascus road; Joshua and the walls of Jericho; Jonah swallowed by a great fish; Daniel and the den of lions; Shadrach and the fiery furnace, and the countless miracles of Jesus. What a sad misconception!

Why is it we think that just because we haven't had an earth-shattering experience that God is not talking to us often and directly? And why do we think that we must be some sort of saint before we could possibly deserve God's time and energy to speak to us?

The fact is God does speak to us often and directly. Some of the ways He speaks are through His word, the Holy Spirit, other godly people, and through circumstances.[2] Many times He is screaming at us! But we don't hear.

The screaming falls on deaf ears for two main reasons. First, we are too busy in our own worlds and consequently we simply don't take time to listen. Second, we have never been taught, and so we don't know how to listen to God.

We Don't Talk

Talking to God is entirely different from listening to God. Most of us pray. Most of us pray whenever it is convenient, or however we have been taught to pray. God doesn't have a problem with all the ways people pray. *We* have problems with praying. The difficulties most of us have with prayer fall into two categories. First, we want immediate results from our prayer, and second, we want an ever-growing closeness with God as a result of each prayer.

In an article in the *Saturday Evening Post*, Robert Schuller says that he prays in five different levels, from positive thinking to actions that bless people. He feels that constant prayer develops our intuition, a level of communication with God that, through His Holy Spirit, penetrates our consciousness. We eventually reach a point when communicating with God where we "know that we know that we know."[3]

So how do we develop a closer relationship with God? How can we feel that our prayers for ourselves and others are more effective?

Communication with God Is Natural

Communication is an endless loop of transmitting and receiving thoughts and ideas. When you enjoy communicating with someone you can feel the thoughts and ideas flow easily between you. The flow of communication is the very foundation for building intimacy. If you have an easy flow of thoughts and ideas, you have a close, intimate relationship.

Communication with God can be as natural as breathing. We can communicate our thoughts, the longings of our hearts, and our most urgent needs.[4] But communicating with God requires changing habits. We can no longer just talk to God. We must communicate with Him as we would our best friend.

Communicating with God builds an intimate relationship with God. It acknowledges His presence and His interaction in our everyday life. Communication with God teaches us that He wants to communicate with us and have fellowship with us. It confirms His desire for goodness in our lives. In turn, through our communication, we grow to be the best we can be. The natural talents we possess, given by Him, come to the forefront of our lives. Using these talents propels us through one success after another because we naturally want to do the best we can. In turn, our success glorifies Him and acknowledges His love for us.

WOW! Isn't that great!

Can We Really Communicate with God?

There are four basic steps in the loop of communicating with God:

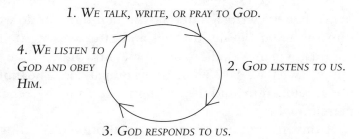

1. We talk, write, or pray to God.
2. God listens to us.
3. God responds to us.
4. We listen to God and obey Him.

The Steps of Communicating with God

We Talk to God

Talking to God is the first part of the communication process. For many of us this is a state of mind we develop when our affairs are in total chaos. Sometimes we talk to God only when there is no one left to talk to. At those times, our talk is seldom honorable. Instead of talking, we complain. The conversation, if you can call it that, is one of disgust, or a futile question such as "Why me?" or "What did I do to deserve this?" spoken when our carefully laid plans are a pile of rubble.

Prayer is one type of talking to God. Prayer is *not* communication. Prayer is but one part of one section of the loop of communication.

There is nothing super spiritual about talking or praying to God. It can be done privately or it can be done publicly. It can be structured by a rigid format, or it can be shot from the hip. Thousands of books have been written, sermons preached, and lessons taught on prayer and talking to God. Thousands more will be taught, preached, and written. That's because prayer works.

But you don't have to talk to communicate with God. You can write to God.

Writing to God makes our prayers materialize onto paper. When we write a letter, how much thought do we put into the letter before, during, and after it is written? By contrast, when we talk to someone, how much thought is put into what we say? There is no comparison. The thought, the visualization, and the feeling make a much deeper impression when we write.

Conversation can become overemotional. Writing, being more deliberate, can become a tool for constant prayer. Unlike vocal prayer, there *is* something super spiritual about writing to God. Something dramatically changes when we put our questions, confusion, emotion, praise or thanksgiving on paper. First, writing takes an investment of time. Second, every time you open your journal, the subject you were writing about jumps back at you and you relive those emotions, questions, and events.

Paul reminds us to *"pray in all kinds of prayers and requests. With this in mind, be alert and always keep on praying for all the saints"* (Ephesians 6:18). David writes, *"I will extol the Lord at all times; his praise will always be on my lips. My soul will boast in the Lord; let the afflicted hear and rejoice"* (Psalm 34:1, 2).

Write your prayers. Writing will engrave in your mind the subjects you talked to God about like a flashing neon sign in the night. Best of all, writing will subconsciously keep you focused on Him instead of on your circumstance. It literally hands the problem or praise over to Him by pulling the emotion out of you and putting it on the paper. Writing it releases it to Him. Does He accept it? Absolutely! Remember, it is Almighty God you are praying to.

CAN WE REALLY COMMUNICATE WITH GOD?

GOD LISTENS TO US IF . . .

Communication is an endless loop of transmitting and receiving thoughts and ideas. For there to be communication, there must be a flow of thoughts and ideas between the transmitter, God, and the receiver, you or vice versa.

But God's listening to us is entirely different. Our self-centered life often attempts to fool us into believing that God always listens to our prayers and requests. God is not under any obligation to listen to us. Throughout the Bible, we learn that a pure heart and a God-centered life are prerequisites for God to listen to us. But no place is it more clear than from David. *"I cried out to him with my mouth; His praise was on my tongue. If I had cherished sin in my heart, the Lord would not have listened; but God has surely listened and heard my voice in prayer"* (Psalm 66:17–19). Paul referred to David as "a man after God's own heart" (Acts 13:22). David spent his entire life striving to understand God's ways and to follow His directions.

A pure heart and a God-centered life is essential to communication with God because everything about God, or that has anything to do with God, is true and good. Nothing evil, dishonest, or not of truth can flow to God because there is no place for it when it gets there! There is nothing evil, dishonest, or untruthful in the kingdom of God. So why should we expect God to listen to us if we lie, cheat, steal, or manipulate? Why should He? Why should He honor our deceit with His time?

That leads us to the real question. Where is the deceit in our heart? It is easy to improve our life on a short term basis. We simply lie, cheat, steal. and manipulate! But does that improve our life on a long term basis? Of course not! But for all of us, at one time or another, the temptation is too great. We are caught in a jam in a relationship. We need to shade or totally discard the truth to negotiate a business deal. We need to hide infidelity from a spouse. We may have committed a crime. The scenarios are as numerous and as individual as we are.

How many of us have resisted temptation and don't have deceit in our heart?

None!

If that is the case, how do we build a relationship with God?

The answer is the basis for the Gospel of Jesus Christ. God sent His Son to be our High Priest, the ultimate sacrifice for our sins. He intercedes for us and brings our hearts and our requests, purified by His blood, to God our Father. God then listens.

Is it possible to continue to talk deceitfully to God after we have acknowledged Christ as our Lord and Savior? Absolutely. But God won't listen. He will lovingly point out our deceit through His discipline, but He won't listen. God listens when our hearts are right. . .plain and simple.

Is it going to be easy to get and keep our hearts right with God?

No. The Christian journey is not a 70 mph ride down the interstate on a clear day in a convertible. It is a stumbling walk along a narrow path with potholes and slippery moss-covered rocks. We stumble when we attempt to talk to God with a deceitful heart. We stumble when we get off the path. We stumble even when we are on the path. For weeks we may walk high on the crest of a hill and see clearly the way to go for miles ahead. Then we may move through a deep valley; often so dark and foggy, that a flashlight shows only the next footstep.

But it is in our stumbling that our Good Shepherd will find us. He will lovingly discipline us through circumstance; and help us get back on the right course. He will also pick us up when we least expect it and don't deserve it. In doing so, He shows us that we can't earn His love. It's a guaranteed gift. When we are on the right course, we come to God with honest questions or requests. And He will listen.

Does that mean God listens only to the saved? Does God ever listen to an honest plea from an unsaved life? For me the answer was a definite Yes! He heard my pleas, then opened doors and created situations to help me seek and find Christ.

Then the adventure began!

> Hear my prayer, O Lord; let my cry for help come to you. Do not hide your face from me when I am in distress. Turn your ear to me; when I call, answer me quickly. (Psalm 102:12).

God Responds to Us

> This is what the Lord says, He who made the earth, the Lord who formed it and established it the Lord is his name: "Call to me and I will answer you and tell you great and unsearchable things you do not know." (Jeremiah 33:23)

When God answers, do you hear? Jesus said, *"He who has ears, let him hear"* (Matthew 11:15). But if all you are using to hear is your ears, then it's a safe bet you haven't heard Him each time He has spoken to you. The more I am open to how God speaks to me, the more I realize how many times I have missed His speaking to me! That's because God speaks to us in many uniquely different ways.

Here are a few of the many ways God speaks to us.

1. His Holy Word. There have been countless times when God's word has leaped off the page to me when I was either exploring or meditating on passages. The timeless wisdom of God's word has personally touched each of us. We have all felt at one time or another that the passage we were reading at a moment of need was meant especially for us. This is one of the mystical facts that make the Bible totally unique.

> *As for God, his way is perfect; the word of the Lord is flawless. He is a shield for all who take refuge in him.* (2 Samuel:22:31)

2. A Ministry. Successful ministries are formed from genuine experiences with God and a desire to fill people's needs as a result of those experiences. There is great power in seeing ourselves through the experiences of other people. The testimony of someone's experience has moved me many times to see a part of my life differently. Someone's ministry has caused me to correct a problem or take action in an area where I sorely needed help.

> *Therefore, if anyone is in Christ, he is a new creation; the old has gone, the new has come! All this is from God, who reconciled us to himself through Christ and gave us the ministry of reconciliation: that God was reconciling the world to himself in Christ, not counting men's sins against them. And he has committed to us the message of reconciliation.* (2 Corinthians 5:17–19)

3. Casual Conversation. Out of the blue, sometimes a subject comes up in conversation that I have prayed about.

This can happen anywhere, anytime, but it always occurs when I least expect it. Suddenly the answer is given to a problem I had asked God's help about earlier. Few things will get our attention the way this answer to prayer will. When this happens to you, you will never forget it.

> *Devote yourselves to prayer, being watchful and thankful. And pray for us, too, that God may open a door for our message, so that we may proclaim the mystery of Christ, for which I am in chains. Pray that I may proclaim it clearly, as I should. Be wise in the way you act toward outsiders; make the most of every opportunity. Let your conversation be always full of grace, seasoned with salt, so that you may know how to answer everyone. (Colossians 26)*

4. *A Touch of Grace.* Grace is God's redemptive love. It acts to draw us to Him and to preserve us in covenant relationship with Him. Grace can also mean kindness or graciousness shown by God. It is a gift, associated with mercy, love, compassion, and patience, that is given by God. There will be acts of God's kindness to us that we neither understand nor feel we deserve.[5]

> *For I am the least of the apostles and do not even deserve to be called an apostle, because I persecuted the church of God. But by the grace of God I am what I am, and his grace to me was not without effect. No, I worked harder than all of them yet not I, but the grace of God that was with me. (1 Corinthians 15:9–10)*

5. *A Dream or Vision.* I drive a lot. Many things come to me while I enjoy quiet in my car or pickup. Dreams and visions are a regular part of my life. I just listen to the quiet

and in a little while it's not quiet anymore.. Can you identify with that?

Daydreams and visions are sparked many times by our being at a certain place at a certain time. We just feel we are supposed to be there. The best thing we could do is just stay there for a while and soak up the whole scene.

> *In the last days, God says, "I will pour out my Spirit on all people. Your sons and daughters will prophesy, your young men will see visions, your old men will dream dreams. Even on my servants, both men and women, I will pour out my Spirit in those days, and they will prophesy.* (Acts 2:17–18)

6. *A Voice.* Not a sound, a voice! Since 1991 I have recorded at least a dozen separate occasions when a voice answered my questions to God or I have been guided by a voice. A voice can shake you to your very soul because you don't necessarily hear it with your ears. You hear it in your mind or your heart, but there is no question that you have been spoken to.

> *The voice of the Lord is over the waters; the God of glory thunders, the Lord thunders over the mighty waters. The voice of the Lord is powerful; the voice of the Lord is majestic. The voice of the Lord breaks the cedars; the Lord breaks in pieces the cedars of Lebanon....The voice of the Lord strikes with flashes of lightning. The voice of the Lord shakes the desert; the Lord shakes the desert of Kadesh.* (Psalm 29:38)

7. *A Gut Feeling.* Better known as a hunch, this is probably the most experienced and least understood way that

God speaks to us. The hunch can come from God or Satan. We must discern the origin of the hunch, depending on how close to God we have grown. It does not come from some trained sixth sense that we have control over. It is not a specialized gift from God that only certain individuals have. There's no problem with God's transmitter. It's our receiver that's not tuned in! We all have hunches. We all have more hunches than we realize. So if we tune into our hunches we will learn to listen more intently and more humbly. When our hunch becomes a true happening, that's when we really begin to notice.

> *We have not received the spirit of the world but the Spirit who is from God, that we may understand what God has freely given us. This is what we speak, not in words taught us by human wisdom but in words taught by the Spirit, expressing spiritual truths in spiritual words. The man without the Spirit does not accept the things that come from the Spirit of God, for they are foolishness to him, and he cannot understand them, because they are spiritually discerned.* (1 Corinthians 2:12–14)

8. *Events or Chains of Events That Guide Us.* Simply put, when a hunch works out right, it makes an impression. We don't know that a chain of events has any significance until we recall and review that they are connected in a way that ultimately leads us in a certain direction. These events do not accidentally happen. In some of my most challenging moments I have looked back at divine events and where they had led me. They gave me the strength to continue to follow the clues God had given me to go in the direction He wanted me to go.

> *Show me your ways, O Lord, teach me your paths; guide me in your truth and teach me, for you are God my Savior, and my hope is in you all day long. Good and upright is the Lord; therefore he instructs sinners in his ways. He guides the humble in what is right and teaches them his way.* (Psalms 25:4–5, 8–9)

WE LISTEN TO GOD IF . . .

This is the critical step in the loop of communication with God. Normally we listen only as a last resort and when all other avenues have failed. We listen only when we are mentally, physically, and emotionally exhausted, when pride and ego are discarded and we face with total honesty the mess we have made of ourselves and our lives. The rock-hard, bottom-line, simple fact is we will not listen to God unless we trust Him. Trust is the foundation of our relationship with Him. Without trust, we play God. We bulldoze through our self-centered lives. We make bad judgments thinking we can handle the situation better than God can.

Now the kind of trust God is looking for is not Sunday morning trust. That's easy. God is looking for Tuesday-morning trust, the real-world, morning-after-Monday, battle-scarred trust.

Trust is where a relationship with God begins to live and function. Without trust there is no obedience. Without trust there is no relationship. Listening and being obedient to God and trusting God go hand in hand. One cannot work without the other.

LISTENING TO GOD + OBEDIENCE = RELATIONSHIP = GOD-CENTERED LIFE
TRUSTING IN GOD

So how do you build trust in God? Ask yourself what has to happen for you to trust someone. What has to happen for you to trust enough to give someone your wallet to take care of? What has to happen for you to trust someone with the keys to your house? What has to happen for you to trust someone with your secrets?

IF I'M GOING TO TRUST YOU COMPLETELY

WITH MY LIFE

I HAVE TO GET TO KNOW YOU

REAL WELL!

David's Trust in God

David teaches many lessons about trust. He says, *"My companion attacks his friends; he violates his covenant. His speech is smooth as butter, yet war is in his heart; his words are more soothing than oil, yet they are drawn sword"* (Psalm 55:20). David is simply saying that talk is cheap. What a person demonstrates is of sole importance. David then writes, *"Cast your cares on the Lord and he will sustain you; he will never let the righteous fall... as for me, I will trust in you"* (Psalm 55:22).

But David's lessons come in more than words. If you have ever had a Bible story read to you as a child, you probably heard the story of David and Goliath. Your mind spun with visions of a young superhero in battle with a giant and winning against all odds.

As you matured into a sophisticated young person, you probably decided that giants went out with Jack and the

Beanstalk. You put David and Goliath in a box up in your mental attic along with other Bible stories such as Samson, Noah, Jonah, Moses, and Joshua. After all, those Bible stories required just too much of a stretch of the imagination. All that unexplainable stuff that happened between 2000 and 4000 years ago wasn't happening now. This was a new era; that old stuff was either explainable or unbelievable—sort of holy fairy tales.

The stories of the Bible are not fairy tales, but we treat them as such. Things might be different if we were taught the lessons that were in each of the stories. But if you were like me, you were taught only the stories.

If you had been taught the lessons, that book of Bible stories would still be on your bedside table. The story of David and Goliath is a tale about the boy David slaying the giant Goliath. The lesson is one of the most practical and powerful lessons in the Bible: how to build communication with God and how to use that communication to slay the Goliaths in your life.

In the early part of the twentieth century in Gainesville, Georgia every morning my mother watched her father and grandfather make their way up Washington Street. Their destination was J. M. Parks and Sons Drygoods, a store that had been thriving on the square since the 1920's. Drygoods, for those under age 50, are goods that aren't wet: clothes and anything having to do with clothes. Marx suits, Stetson hats, Indian Head fabric, Arrow shirts, and the very popular Peter's Shoes. Now the Peter's Shoe company had a promotional team to help advertise their product. One of the things they did was to place an empty shoe that belonged to Robert, a member of the promotional team, on top of the cash register and fill it full of cotton seeds. The person who guessed the number of cotton seeds in the shoe won a pair

Robert Wadlow, Tallest Man in the World.

of Peter's shoes. People thought that all they had to do was get a shoe the same size, fill it full of cotton seeds, and then count them to get the right number. The trouble was you couldn't find a shoe the same size as Robert's.

Robert was a celebrity. He received royal treatment when he came to Gainesville. The Princeton Hotel gave him the whole second floor. Not necessarily because they wanted to. They had to. And not because of some fine print in the promotional contract, but because Robert had to sleep in the hallway of the second floor on four beds laid side by side.

Robert Wadlow was a celebrity because he was entered in the Guinness Book of Records as the tallest man in the world. His shoe size was 37AA. He weighed 439 pounds and stood 8 feet and 11 inches tall, approximately six inches shorter than Goliath.[6]

David's Communication with God

The story of David and Goliath is found in 1 Samuel 17. The author introduces David into the Bible with a bang. Within three chapters, a total of five pages, David goes from nonexistence to being anointed by Samuel as the chosen successor to Saul, the first king of Israel. After the unprecedented victory over the giant Goliath, he became the most popular celebrity in the country. David's name was mentioned alongside Saul's whenever there was talk of the Israelites' victories in battle. Saul was less secure in the Lord than David. All this sprouting popularity for one of his subjects made Saul very jealous. He worried that David might overthrow his throne. The worry and jealousy grew to hatred. The hatred spawned an obsessive unsuccessful campaign to hunt David down like an animal.

David had seven older brothers. His relationship with his brothers was not a tranquil one. It's a safe bet they didn't understand why the prophet Samuel had anointed David instead of one of them to be the next king. As the story goes, young David was sent by his father, Jesse, to take food to three of his brothers who were at the battlefront, fighting with the Israelites against the Philistines. It's no wonder that David's arrival was met with a cool welcome. They scoffed at his duties as a shepherd. They did what they could to belittle him, and showed no appreciation for the food he had brought them.

David had obviously heard all this before. He bristled back a response of his own in typical sibling rivalry fashion. At that point, David overheard the soldiers report that King Saul would reward with great wealth the person who would kill the Philistine, Goliath. David wasted no time volunteering his services to Saul.

Saul was not impressed. He reminded David that he was but a boy, no match for a seasoned warrior twice his size. But David had an answer. This answer is the turning point of the story. It is also the turning point of *your* story. No more Goliaths. No more Red Seas in front of you. No more walls of Jericho blocking you. No more chains and shackles imprisoning you. The answer is found in 1 Samuel 17:34. David said:

> *Your servant has been keeping his father's sheep. When a lion or a bear came and carried off a sheep from the flock, I went after it, struck it and rescued the sheep from its mouth. When it turned on me, I seized it by its hair, struck it and killed it. Your servant has killed both the lion and the bear; this uncircumcised Philistine will be like one of them, because he has defied the armies of the living God. The Lord*

who delivered me from the paw of the lion and the paw of the bear will deliver me from the hand of this Philistine. (1 Samuel 17:34)

This one sentence contains two fundamental principles for building communication with God. If you develop an understanding of these two principles and use them on a daily basis, you will notice an astounding improvement in your relationship with God. You will enjoy trusting His wisdom; and you will experience His ability to obliterate any obstacle in your path without your lifting a finger.

PRINCIPLE NUMBER ONE:
To build communication with God, you must spend time alone with God to talk to Him and listen to Him on a one-on-one basis.

Over one-third the Old Testament was written by David or was written about David. Yet David's killing the lion and the bear was recorded only once. No one else saw the killing. It was not important for anyone else to see the killing. It was only important for David to see the killing.

When God wants your undivided attention, He doesn't need an audience. He doesn't want one. He wants you to be alone with Him. When you want God's attention, you don't need an audience. You want Him to be alone with you.

As a boy David was a shepherd. He spent countless nights alone with his flock of sheep. With seven older brothers, he probably welcomed the nights alone. While David was alone in the wilderness, he was put in situations that required his total reliance on God. David probably faced many unrecorded perils: situations that built his faith and taught him how to talk to God and how to listen to God's guidance.

David recorded his praises and his pleas to God through his songs, many of which are recorded in the book of Psalms. His harp became a symbol of his poetic dexterity. David was introduced into Saul's court as a gifted musician. There he sang praises to God with the music he had created alone as a shepherd. David's psalms were a constant reminder to him of how God had interacted in his life.

There are many instances in the Bible and throughout history, where the raw metal in good people has been forged into razor sharp steel by situations that required a period of time alone with God. Moses was in Midian for forty years before he went back to Egypt to free his people. Paul left Damascus to be alone in Arabia for two years after his conversion on the Damascus road. Jesus was alone in the desert when He was tempted by Satan. Poor Jonah was alone with God in the belly of a fish for three days. Noah was alone in a crowd. For approximately one hundred years, while he was building the ark, he was probably ridiculed and ostracized by the people who knew him.

Being alone with God is a key ingredient before we can begin astounding careers .

Chuck Colson, after his indictment for his activities in Watergate, spent seven months in prison. His time alone with God guided him to form Prison Fellowship Ministries. The US Prison Fellowship movement now includes a staff of approximately 300 and some 50,000 members.

Dave Dravecky, pitcher for the San Francisco Giants, was diagnosed with a cancerous tumor in his pitching arm in the fall of 1988. His time alone with God gave him the strength to make an inspiring comeback to pitch again in the major leagues in the summer of 1989. Later that same year, Dravecky broke his pitching arm twice: once while pitching and once celebrating when the Giants won the National League Championship.

In October of 1989, doctors told Dave that cancer had probably recurred in his arm. Dave announced his retirement one month later. His pitching arm was amputated in 1990. Dave now travels telling his story of how God gave him the strength to carry on.

Joni Eareckson Tada, paralyzed from a diving accident in 1967, saw her life change in a split second. Her time alone with God transformed her imprisoned life in a wheelchair to a productive enterprise as a painter, speaker, and writer. She is now founder of JAF ministries for the disabled.

Even though Bill McCartney was head football coach of the University of Colorado, his personal trials forced him to be alone with God for countless years. In March of 1990, on a trip to Pueblo, Colorado, Bill conceived the idea "Promise Keepers," a ministry totally committed to building Godly men. He remained head coach for four more years. During that time, Colorado finished number one in the nation after the 1991 season and went to nine postseason bowl games in ten years. Bill McCartney resigned as head football coach in November of 1994 when the team was ranked in the top five in the nation. "Promise Keepers" has grown to be the number one men's Christian organization in the country.

PRINCIPLE NUMBER TWO:
In order to face and overcome the challenges awaiting you in the future, you must remember the things God did for you in the past.

David knew God protected him from the lion and the bear. David knew God would protect him from Goliath. I bet if it were known, David could recall many times when God routed him away from the cobra or the scorpion. David could also tell you of mysterious hunches telling him where to find a lost lamb, or the best path to take his flock.

Remember that it was David's victory over Goliath that initiated his popularity in Israel. As David's popularity grew, King Saul felt that his throne was being threatened. Saul's insecurity grew to obsessive jealousy of David's popularity. It became Saul's mission to kill David because he was a threat to his throne. David had to listen to God's guidance and direction many times while he was running for his life from Saul. As David remembered the hunches he had when he was a shepherd, he understood that God was intervening in his life, guiding and directing him along the path to safety from Saul (1 Samuel 19).

David's life was a constant recollection of what God did for him. David faithfully praised God and sang psalms of thanksgiving glorifying Him. He was continually recalling and recording through his poetry God's intervention in his life.

So how do we remember the things God has done for us in the past?

Remembering the big things God does is easy. But most of the time God's ways are little ways. The big things He does are almost always a complex culmination of little things He does.

Remembering God's little ways is not easy. Many times daily complexities overshadow the still small voice talking to us, or the situation that put us at the right place at the right time. And don't forget the power of this world, Satan, who doesn't want you to remember any of the little ways God works to intervene in our lives.

Recording is the key. One of the methods David recorded the ways God intervened in his life was through his music. But most of us aren't poets or musicians. Still, building communication with God requires some type of tool for recording everything you and God do together. If we don't record, we are likely to forget . . . out of sight, out of mind. (Satan always wants us to forget). As you record . . . and later review . . . God's interventions in your life, you will see how He is leading you toward His will for you.

So let's explore one way you can learn how to communicate with God.

---

[1] Staff, "Restoring the Book to the Rose," *USA Today,* August 1994, 16.
[2] Dr. Charles Stanley, *How to Listen to God* (Nashville, Tenn: Thomas Nelson, Inc., 1985), pp. 7–18.
[3] Robert H. Schuller, "How I Pray," *Saturday Evening Post*, March 1995, p. 36.
[4] 4. Jan Johnson, "Turning your thoughts into prayers," *Discipline Journal,* July 1996, 91.
[5] Herbert Lockyer, Sr. *Illustrated Bible Dictionary* (Nashville, Tenn: Thomas Nelson, 1986) p. 443.
[6] *Guinness Book of Records* (Enfield, England: Guinness Publishing Ltd., 1966) p.9

PART TWO

LEARNING HOW TO COMMUNICATE WITH GOD

The Journal

A communication journal is the tool we use to learn how to talk to God and how to listen to God. It is a record of the course of events, natural or supernatural, that guide us to:

1. Discover our God-given talents.
2. Learn how to use these talents.
3. Live out the purpose of our life by using these talents.

The journal is also a record of our questions to God and His answers to us about every factor of our life. The beauty of a communication journal is that it becomes a personal document of proof that God is very real, He has a wonderful destination for us, He plans events for us that help us get to our destination, and finally He plans events that are for our good.

I want to repeat something very important. Remembering the big things God does for you is easy, but remembering God's little ways is not easy. Yet, almost always the big things He does are a complex culmination of the little things He does.

God has a place for each of us in His big picture. It involves using our talents and developing a purpose for our life. God is constantly giving us opportunities to seek His guidance in many forms to help us reach our highest potential. The higher the potential we reach, the more we glorify Him and amplify His presence on earth.

The Nuts and Bolts

My first journal consisted of a spiralbound notebook. When I look back at its tattered pages, through the scribbled images and through the printed notes of a shaking hand, I see questions from my heart. I see pain and distress. I see confusion. I see praise and thanksgiving. I see victories and defeat. I also see that it made no difference to God if I was writing on the back of a paper bag! I was writing to Him. That's all that mattered.

I was talking to my Father in heaven who was dedicated to my prosperity and well-being. I was talking to my Father in heaven who was infinitely wise, infinitely understanding, and infinitely loving. I was talking to my Father in heaven who wanted to listen.

In September of 1991, I visited my son in Miami, Florida., who was studying architecture at Miami Dade College. The next morning he "invited" me to go shopping. Never go shopping with an architecture student! God doesn't make wallets thick enough and credit cards don't have enough 00000s. What a store! I was impressed! My checkbook wasn't. But I found a section with logs, records, all kinds of books of all sizes with either blank pages or pages with lines. These were hard-bound books with formal, dressy covers with either artwork or gold-inlaid leather. The book I bought has been my communication journal since that day.

I look back in my old journal frequently. I see questions from my heart. I see pain and distress. I see confusion. I see praise and thanksgiving. I see victories and defeat. I see scribbled notes from a more peaceful hand. I see it makes no difference to God whether or not I am writing on the back of a paper bag! I am writing to Him. That's all that matters.

For starters, buy something simple. Then after you get in a groove, move up to something more permanent, for this will become your legacy. Be sure it will be sturdy enough to stand a century of reading. Someone . . . or maybe thousands . . . may be led to Christ because of your experiences that you have left in writing.

> *The nations will fear the name of the Lord, all the kings of the earth will revere your glory. For the Lord will rebuild Zion and appear in his glory. He will respond to the prayer of the destitute; he will not despise their plea. Let this be written for a future generation, that a people not yet created may praise the Lord.* (Psalm 102:15–18).

IN DIARY FORM WRITE TO GOD:

A) **Your requests**
- Your needs, wants, desires, both tangible and intangible
- Why do you want them?
- What good are they to you, your family, and others?

Ask and it will be given to you; seek and you will find; knock and the door will be opened to you. For everyone who asks receives; he who seeks finds; and to him who knocks, the door will be opened. Which of you, if his son asks for bread, will give him a stone? Or if he asks for a fish, will give him a snake? If you, then, though you are evil, know how to give good gifts to your children, how much more will your Father in heaven give good gifts to those who ask him! (Matt.7:7–11)

B) **Your hurts and complaints**
- What hurt are you feeling?
- Why are you hurting?
  -Be honest; That may be difficult
  -We don't like seeing the truth about us in writing.
  -Remember who you are talking to.

O Lord, hear my prayer, listen to my cry for mercy; in your faithfulness and righteousness come to my relief. (Psalm 143:1)

C) **Your confusions**
- Questions about your life and where you are headed.
  -Which fork in the road do I take?
- Ask for a sign
  -When you get one and it is not clear enough, ask for another one.

Let the morning bring me word of your unfailing love, for I have put my trust in you. Show me the way I should go, for to you I lift up my soul. (Psalm 143:8)

D) **His answers**
"Because he loves me," says the Lord, "I will rescue him; I will protect him, for he acknowledges my name. He will call upon me, and I will answer him; I will be with him in trouble, I will deliver him and honor him." (Psalm 91:1415)

E) **Your thanks for:**
- Answers to prayer
- Touches of grace
- Blessings out of the blue
- Victories
- Divine guidance, simultaneous events, or chains of events that lead you out of a disaster or into a blessing
- Defeats—you learn twice as much from your failures as from your successes.

You are my God, and I will give you thanks; you are my God, and I will exalt you. Give thanks to the Lord, for he is good; his love endures forever." (Psalm 118:28–29)

Some Tips and Suggestions

Use key words for reference. Here is a suggested list of key words. Use them at the beginning of an entry to identify what the entry is about. It makes your record far more organized and more fun to review. Write the key words in the left hand margin so they stand out:

- Question
- Guidance
- Dream
- Event
- Hunch

- Blessing
- Complaint

There are many times when we simply forget to write or reflect on some event after it unfolds. When we look back and see how some things fit (hunches, chain of events), it's incredibly uplifting to write an overview of how you have been guided, or protected by God. In these instances, use a word like *overview* or *reflection*.

Be up close and personal with God

When I began my communication journal, I began each entry with the word "Father." As I watched my relationship grow with Him, and I saw just how much He was working in my life, I changed my beginnings. Instead of beginning with "Father" now, when it is guidance or a blessing, I write "Thank You Father" no explanation necessary.

How God Speaks to Us and Answers Our Questions: A Review

    His Holy Word
       2 Samuel 22:31
    A Ministry
       Acts 6:25
    Casual conversation
       Colossians 4:26
    A touch of grace
       1 Corinthians: 15:9–10
    A dream or vision
       Acts 2:1718
    A voice
       Psalm 29:38
    A gut feeling
       1 Corinthians 2:10–14
    Events or chains of events that guide us
       Psalm 25:45, 89

How to Get God Really Excited about Your Life

The more I used my journal, the more I listened. But listening is not the key. Doing is the key. First you listen to what God says. The you do what He says. Don't expect Him to speak to you for long if you just listen and don't start doing.

If your stock broker made you a million dollars, you would do with your money what he told you to do, wouldn't you? If your boss doubled the size of your workspace over the next six years and also doubled your income, you would do your work the way he told you to do it, wouldn't you?

The communication journal is a tool to listen to what God wants you to do in all areas of your life. It is also a tool to listen to what God wants you not to do in some areas right now. Timing is everything. No one knows this better than Jesus Christ!

After I had used my journal for a while, it dawned on me how stupid I had been to press forward on some worthy project when God had not given me the go ahead. I may have had a dozen questions written to Him. I was trying to move on all twelve when only three had the green light! The other areas were silent. I might have missed this if I had not recorded the questions earlier. God was telling me the one word believers hate to hear when they are banging on His door—wait! God tells us to wait on a specific problem many times by simply not answering us. We may feel rejection. We may experience impatience. But He is telling us is to wait.

Waiting requires superior obedience. How long did Noah wait? How long did the Jews wait under Pharaoh? How long did Moses wait? Waiting takes overcoming an emotion such as "Lord, I'm tired of this! I'm taking things into my own hands. I'm doing it my way, now!"

Waiting requires superior obedience; but it also brings superior results. The best analogy I can use is the great American pastime, football. The quarterback waits for the exact moment to pass the ball to the receiver who is also waiting for the exact split second to leap into the air to catch it. The return man waits for his blockers to form a "v" or a wall, to guide him up the field toward the opponent's goal line. If the return man waits and his blockers wait to make the right block, a lot of yards, possibly a touchdown, are gained. If the return man doesn't wait for his wall of blockers, a 250-pound defensive back squashes him into the dirt.

How many times have you not waited and gotten out in front of the blockers God assigned to guide and protect you? How many times have you said, "If only I had just waited." Get God excited about you. Do what He says do when He says do it. Wait when He says wait.

Give to Him

One day the boss calls you into his office, spends some time reviewing your past year's performance, then shakes your hand and gives you an envelope. In it is a big fat raise! You worked hard for it and you deserve it, but you weren't expecting it. Let's be optimistic and say it's a raise of $5/hour. You have a million places you can put the money. How easy would it be to give ten cents back to God? But why give it to God?

The boss didn't give the raise to you. God gave it to you through your boss. God could have just as easily given you $3.50/hour instead of a $5.00. But He gave you $5.00. So what are you going to do? Are you going to give some of it back to Him?

And what about the other blessings God bestows? What are you going to do with an unexpected store discount, tax refund, windfall, or some other blessing out of the blue? How many hints will God have to give you before you begin participating in the one law that unleashes the abundance He has waiting for you? Or will you be so locked into your own world that you will never participate at all?

> *Give, and it shall be given to you. A good measure, pressed down, shaken together and running over, will be poured into your lap. For with the measure you use, it will be measured to you.* (Luke 6:38)

God gives and you can't outgive Him. This is a beautiful truth. It is a favorite testimony of individuals who have taken on a private challenge to see if they could outgive God. Journals are loaded with stories of blessings out of the blue. They come in the strangest ways, at the most needed times, in the craziest of situations. They come in ways we don't know and do not understand.

The sad fact is that the majority of us either are ignorant of this truth or aren't thankful enough to acknowledge the Giver with a portion of the gift back in return. In not doing so we cut ourselves off from the flow of abundance so vast it is beyond our comprehension.

Did it ever occur to you that to give out of a blessing doesn't cause any harm to you? Look at it this way. Our Father in heaven wants us to enjoy the abundance He has in store for us. So what does He do? In order to get us started He first gives us a gift. Out of that unexpected gift He simply wants us to honor Him by giving Him part of it back. But what do most of us do? We run off and blow the gift on our own indulgence!

The Twisted Truth

Unfortunately some people use this truth the wrong way. People have mistakenly used this verse as a fund-raising technique for either themselves or their church. The rationale was that God *had* to respond to our gifts. Nothing could be farther from the truth.

We are not the center of the universe. God does not have to respond to our commands or our bribes, which is exactly what our gift becomes when we are giving to God in order to receive. In effect we are saying: "It is written in the Bible that if we give, you will give back to us more. So here it is. Now where's mine?"

This is a futile attempt to manipulate God to give us more of what we give to Him.

God is not an investment broker. He is not required to give us a return on our investment in Him. Moreover, manipulation is deceit. When we attempt to manipulate God, we are trying to play God; telling Him what we want Him to do. And so we arrive full circle back to the first requirement for our communication with God: If there is deceit in our heart, He will not listen.

God will respond to our gifts of reverence and thanksgiving, not to our attempts at manipulation. He will respond in whatever fashion He desires, at His own timing.

"In whatever fashion He desires" is the key. We don't know how He will respond. We don't know the big picture. His infinite wisdom knows our exact present need and our future needs. We seldom can correctly diagnose our present needs, much less our needs in the future!

The Guarantee

But there is a guarantee that we must rely on with the faith of a little child. Paul plainly states it in Romans 8:26–28:

> *In the same way, the Spirit helps us in our weakness. We do not know what we ought to pray for, but the Spirit himself intercedes for us with groans that words cannot express. And he who searches our hearts knows the mind of the spirit, because the Spirit intercedes for the saints in accordance with God's will. And we know that in all things God works for the good of those who love him, who have been called according to his purpose."* (Romans 8:28)

Trying to understand God's ways is one of our great adventures of life. It is the key to our spiritual growth, our ever-evolving wisdom, and our growing relationship with Jesus Christ. So give to Him and He will give back to you, pressed down, shaken together, and in ways you will be completely challenged to understand.

Test Him

Whenever you get a monetary blessing {or one you can put a monetary value on}, record it in your communication journal. Then give at least a tithe from the blessing.

What will happen? The richest and wisest man ever to walk the face of the earth, other than Jesus Christ, King Solomon, said it best:

> *Trust in the Lord with all your heart and lean not on your own understanding; in all ways acknowledge him, and he will make your paths straight. Do not be wise in your own eyes; fear the Lord and shun evil. This will bring health to your body and nourishment to your bones. Honor the Lord with your wealth, with the first fruits of all your crops; then your barns will be filled to overflowing, and your vats will brim over with new wine.* (Proverbs 3:5–10)

God doesn't care that you get started with 10%. He only cares that you get started.

Examples from My Journal

I'd like to share some examples from my journal. I have found that when I share examples it takes the mystery out of starting something new. Sometimes it is the nudge someone needs to get started. Other times it reinforces the commitment to build a journal.

There are days I find myself rushed, and I throw in a small notation so I can expand on it at a later date. There are days when the whole overview of a set of events becomes crystal clear and I want to take the time to record it with more detail. But the important thing is to *write something down!*

When times were their toughest my journal has been my best friend. I could open the pages and recall how God listened to me, answered me, and guided me through my most trying experiences. Here are a few examples:

> BLESSING/GUIDANCE, October 6, 1991: I was on my second or third date with Maggie. I had reserved tickets for an Amy Grant concert. When I went to pick up the tickets, something told me to ask if any better seats had been turned in. There were. They turned out to be the best seats in the house. This may be trivial, but thank you, Father.
>
> BLESSING/GUIDANCE, August 30, 1992: If I had not been in the grocery store at the right time and I if had not been in the fruit section, I would have not run into Anita. I would have not known that she still needed a commercial dishwasher for her new restaurant. I had talked to her husband a month earlier and he had told me to wait a year. Anita wants it now! I schedule another meeting with her next week. Thank you, Father!

GUIDANCE, September 10, 1992: Father, over the last two years I have had many questions concerning whether I should stay in my business. This week I lost four major accounts, but I gained three leads and one new account at the same time. It's just enough for me to feel that you are telling me to keep rebuilding my company.

REFLECTION, December 31,1993. Father, I have waited on You and I have been rewarded. I have witnessed a perfect timing of events to the extent no one would believe unless they were beside me.

- The leap of faith in marrying Sara.
- The perfect times we have enjoyed.
- The nurturing we have done for each other.
- Money arriving at the perfect time for taxes, my children, bills, etc.
- My condo renting in minutes.
- My car selling in hours.

You protected me and my company. You gave me time to rest, and you gave me time to glorify You. Thank You.

GUIDANCE, January 15, 1994, Our second Sunday school a First Presbyterian. In the class I was in, anyone could teach any time they wanted to. I had been wanting to teach but didn't know how to break through the red tape. This is made to order. Thank you.

BLESSING, March 7, 1994: I was working in my warehouse in Myrtle Beach wondering what to do. Business and bills were tough. Should I leave or stay?

My landlord shows up unannounced and volunteers to reduce my space and rent in half at his expense. Thank You, Father!

HUNCH, March 23, 1994: I left my office in Simpsonville to see some clients. Something told me to go back because I thought I had left something. I pull into my parking lot to find the Duke Power man there to cut off my power. I had forgotten to pay my bill! I wrote him a check and he left on the power. Thank you, Father.

COMPLAINT, June 1, 1994: Father, I have prayed to you often that I was tired and I asked you for a sign what to do. Sara and I went to Ryan's Steak House for lunch. I had not been in a Ryan's in two years. While we were eating, a family comes in to sit at a large table next to us. The family had three handicapped children. One was a palsied child about 25 years old. They were very loving to their children, but you could see the exhaustion in their eyes. I am no longer tired Father. Thank you.

EVENT, June 7, 1994: After nineteen years of silence I was invited to speak to the men's group of my warehouse manager's church. It was the first time I had spoken since 1975. I was literally busting at the seams, eager to tell what You have done for me. Now they want me to speak to whole congregation for two Sundays! Thank you, Father.

HELP, September 10, 1994: Father, I don't know how I'm going to schedule all I need to do. You always come through just in time. Thank you.

HUMOR, September 17, 1995: Sara and I are in two cars on the way to our cabin in North Georgia. I was going too fast, but so was the truck about a

¼ mile in front of me. We go over a hill and come face to face with a state trooper. He gets the truck in front of me. Thank you, Father!

GUIDANCE/EVENT, October 22, 1995: I graduate from Christian Financial Concepts. We are told not to go home and promote our services; but to let God guide and promote our work. In my class is a man from Greenville, Bob Heitz. He is good friends with the associate minister in my church! Wow! Double exposure! I started to work immediately.

OVERVIEW, April 29, 1996: Mother is five days out of surgery. She has a good attitude. She is strapped in an armadillo-style sheet of armor around her neck. It is a system of white plastic plates held together with velcro-like tape that puts a viselike grip on her neck. If I hadn't followed my hunch and hired two men instead of just one back in March, I would not have been able to leave for Florida so easily. I didn't have the money, but you gave me the signs to hire them. I am so very thankful.

PLEA, June 19, 1996: Father, I don't know what's happening, but it's coming down in buckets. It looks like a dam-up of problems and situations. Give me the cool to keep my head on straight. This has been a rugged week. I've driven many miles with little sleep. I am worn out. I need Your touch. Thank you.

The Legacy of Your Record

Who will read your communication journal? Who will be led to Christ because of your experiences? Who will rededicate their lives to Christ because of reading your personal record? What family will you have held together? What life will you have changed?

In total reverence to God, I ask you the following question: How much more thirsty can you make someone for the word of God written 2000 years ago if you have examples of God's word in action written this past week?

Maybe that family you hold together will be your children's. Maybe the person you lead to Christ will be your employer or your key employee. Maybe it will be a close relative. Maybe that person will become a leader in our government. Maybe that person is there already.

There will soon come days of unexplained tremendous gratification when your efforts to improve your communication with God will be rewarded. The first of many of those days will happen after only a few written pages in your communication journal. Goliaths will be conquered, Red Seas will be crossed, walls will come tumbling down, and someone will look at you in spellbound amazement when you share your personal stories of God's supernatural power working in your life. Some of the greatest rewards I have received are the stories of lives that were touched when I taught this subject.

Seek His kingdom. Seek a true working relationship with Him. Honor Him with the first fruits of your sweat and accomplishments. Honor Him by also recording what He has done for you each day. And all these things will be granted unto you.

A Gentle Reminder

I want to remind you of something: the power of events or chains of events that guide us.

Simply put, when a hunch "works out right" it makes an impression. We don't know that a chain of events has any significance until we recall and review that they are connected in a way that ultimately leads us in a certain direction. These events do not happen accidentally.

In some of my most challenging moments I have looked back at divine events and where they had led me. They gave me the strength to continue to follow the clues that God had given me to go in the direction He wanted me to go.

As I was finishing this manuscript, I was looking back in my journal to select examples. Little did I know that during my research I would get a closer glimpse of God's guidance in my life over the last nine years.

Here is a list of the more obvious events, totally orchestrated by God, that have guided me to form the ministry of Skyhook:

1. May 1987: I gave my life and my company to Christ.
2. January 6, 1988: I joined AA.
3. September 27, 1989: Half of my company was destroyed by Hurricane Hugo when it hit South Carolina.
4. January–December 1990: Half of what remained of my company collapsed during the recession of 1990.
5. January 1991: I began picking up aluminum cans as a humility exercise to listen to God's guidance by taking care of little things before I could take care of big things.
6. April 1991: I began my communication journal.
7. October 1991: I attended a Christian Financial Concepts weekend seminar to research ways to help my situation.
8. June 23, 1993: I was given a God-directed marriage. The romance had begun several months earlier when I met Sara.

9. January 15, 1994: Sara and I found a Sunday school where I could teach on a volunteer basis.
10. June 7, 1994: I spoke for the first time in 19 years to a men's group at Fountain of Life Pentecostal Holiness Church, Piedmont, South Carolina.
11. July 1994: People waited in line to rent my former home at a time when a better cash flow was crucial.
12. April 1995: People waited in line to buy my home without my having to list it.
13. October 22, 1995: I received my accreditation as a Christian Financial Concepts counselor.
14. December 31, 1995: My company completed its first profitable year since Hurricane Hugo.
15. December 1995: I began teaching Sunday school at my church on a regular basis.
16. March 1996: Although it made no financial sense at all, I hired one additional emergency repair person for my company.
17. April 1996: My mother was paralyzed from a boating accident in Florida. I am an only child. To be with her I left my company for an extended period of time for the first time since 1989.
18. May 1996: I was in Myrtle Beach on business. A book at Barnes and Noble literally leapt off the shelf. I realized it was God's way of telling me to begin a speaking career for Him. It was the first book I needed to teach me how to begin a speaking career.
19. July 1996: I call a Christian speakers' bureau and ask how I can get started.

20. November 1996: I traveled to Miami and began my education so I could qualify for a Christian speakers bureau to represent me.
21. March 1997: To free up my time I hired my third emergency repair person.
22. June 1997: I formed Skyhook—a ministry that teaches people how to let God help them find their talents, finance their life, and fund their church.
23. October 1997: Half of my time is now in my ministry with my employees handling the day-to-day operations.
24. I have cold-called a total of only three days over seven years. My company grew an average of 15 percent per year.
25. Our company is an 18-hour-a-day, seven-day-a-week restaurant service business. Through the years, whenever I needed a rest or when there was a family emergency, God gave me the time to rest or to do whatever was needed. Mysteriously there would be no service calls during these periods. Also, Sunday service calls averaged one or two per year.

PART THREE

THE MINISTRY OF S★YHOOK

Statement of Faith

I, Fred Parks Morris, believe in God the Father Almighty, Maker of heaven and earth.

And in Jesus Christ, His only Son, our Lord; who was conceived by the Holy Ghost, born of the Virgin Mary, suffered under Pontius Pilate, was crucified, dead, and buried. He descended into hell. The third day He rose again from the dead. He ascended into heaven, and sitteth on the right hand of God the Father Almighty; from thence He shall come to judge the quick and the dead.

I believe in the Holy Ghost, the holy catholic Church, the communion of saints, the forgiveness of sins, the resurrection of the body, and the life everlasting.

I also believe that He is the Creator of my own personality, my talents, my personal abundance, and all the wealth of the Universe. I believe that He shows me my talents and guides me to develop them to my highest potential. It then becomes my responsibility to use the blessings He bestows on me to glorify Him and not myself. This is one way I can acknowledge that He is the one true God, Lord and Ruler of the Universe.

About the Founder

Fred Morris, speaker, writer, consultant, teaches how to get results from practical, Christian communication with God. He is recognized as an experienced teacher on topics including: *Nine Steps for Managing God's Wealth*, *The Superpower of Humility*, and *Sharpening your Listening-to-God Skills*.

While over 1,000,000 businesses declared bankruptcy in 1996, Fred watched his company, shattered in 1989, become rebuilt by the hands of God to be virtually debt free in 1997.

Fred is an accomplished speaker. His honors include the Trustee's Gold Medal from Clemson as the University's best speaker. His style encompasses numerous inspiring personal stories in order to touch as many people as possible.

Fred stresses practical Christianity. As he puts it, "the kind of stuff that gets you through the Tuesdays and Wednesdays when it comes down in buckets."

Fred is president of American Distributing Industries, Inc., manufacturer of water-based detergents and power cleaning systems. He is a certified Christian financial counselor, and helps people with credit problems to rebuild their financial life according to the word of God.

Fred has been a member of First Presbyterian Church, Greenville, South Carolina since 1993. He still enjoys close ties with his Methodist roots and also has active associations with Baptist, Pentecostal, and other evangelical churches. Fred is also a member of *Fellowship of Companies for Christ International* and *Christian Leaders and Authors Speakers Services*.

After his company was destroyed by Hurricane Hugo in 1989, and rebuilt by the hands of God, Fred founded Skyhook, a church-building ministry that teaches how to let God help you find your talents, finance your life and fund your church.

Skyhook was founded to teach people how to let God help them.
"The most expensive thing people own is their ego," Fred says. "The most costly thing people do is anything alone. Surrendering your life to Jesus Christ is not losing your identity. It is quite the opposite. It finds your identity!"

Let the supernatural power of God help you find your talents.
The vast majority of people have no idea what their true talents are. Worldly pressures such as seeking the job with the most money or security keep talents locked up inside where they are never used. Abundance and security are found through Jesus Christ. When we find Him, He then helps us find ourselves and our God-given talents. We are able to use these talents to achieve a level of excellence that enables us to naturally glorify Him without any extra effort of our part.

One of the key adventures of life is the search for understanding why He gives us what He gives us at the time He decides to give it. Rest assured He will give it. We must simply follow a few guidelines.

Let the supernatural power of God help you finance your life.

Many people consider a good stock broker and a good banker as two essential ingredients needed to finance their wants and needs. But few of us consider having our lives financed by Jesus Christ. Could it be that He might not approve of the things we buy or invest in? We might be surprised. He wants us to have the desires of our hearts. As long as our hearts are in the right place, the ultimate Financier will meet the needs of our life, our family, and our business in whatever fashion He desires and according to His divine timing. Rest assured His timing will be perfect. What He gives, and the amount He gives will be perfect. It will be for our greatest good— either immediately or over the long haul. We must simply follow a few guidelines.

Let the supernatural power of God help you fund your church.

God's people must be taught how to apply His word in their everyday lives. His word must be taught in a language that is used six days a week—not just on Sunday. The "*God said it, I believe it, that settles it*" approach works great on Sunday. But they do not believe it works for the other six days a week. The church body must be taught in a practical, step-by-step manner how God's word works in their everyday lives, *especially in the area of wealth*. Then and only then will the church body fund its church as a matter of natural habit.

Jesus Christ will help us find our talents and guide us in the best use of our talents. Jesus Christ will guide us to the abundance needed to finance our lives. He will guide us to the resources we need to fund our church.

Current Speaking Topics

NINE STEPS FOR MANAGING GOD'S WEALTH
(6 to 7-hour presentation)

This in-depth Scripture-loaded program covers how God cycles wealth through our lives and how we can both manage and enjoy the wealth He gives us.

In order for us to develop a truly successful attitude about managing God's wealth, we must:

1. Understand completely that He is the sole creator of wealth.
2. Learn and apply the laws He has provided for us to manage and build wealth.
3. Trust Him with all our heart and not rely on our own understanding.

Then we can gain a greater ability to see the difference between the way God manages wealth and the way the world manages wealth. Do you know the answer to these questions?

- How does the world's attitude stop us from reaching our highest potential?
- How does God's word answer our personal financial questions?
- What roadblocks do we have between us and God's wealth?
- How can we easily build our trust in God?
- How can we maintain a cheerful attitude about giving?
- Where did today's great motivational laws and techniques originate?
- Under what conditions does God allow us to build a surplus?

You will leave this program with a far deeper knowledge and understanding of God's ways for managing His wealth. You will attain far greater faith and confidence to let God guide you and help you finance your life in all your endeavors.

HOW TO SHARPEN YOUR LISTENING-TO-GOD SKILLS
(A 60-minute keynote or two-hour presentation with break)

This program is designed to increase dramatically the stewardship participation of a church body and teach individuals a step-by-step method for building communication with God.

1. The foundation of stewardship is your relationship with God.
2. The foundation of your relationship with God is communication.
3. The foundation of communication is listening.

Once you teach a group how to listen effectively to God, you elevate that group's relationship with God. At the same time, you elevate their church to a level of stewardship that becomes a natural habit instead of an added chore.

Enjoy some of Fred's personal stories while you learn:

- Why we don't communicate with God effectively.
- The four steps of communicating with God.
- The little ways God talks to us.
- The wrong way we look at Bible stories.
- David's two principles for building communication with God.
- The journal: the best tool for building communication with God.
- How to build a communication journal.
- How to use the communication journal to build a stewardship program in your church.

Fred has received many unsolicited letters from excited participants who have put his principles to work. As you begin to notice the little ways God is speaking to you, you will truly agree that you have sharpened your listening-to-God skills.

How to Become a Christian Entrepreneur
(60-minute presentation)

The testimony of Fred Parks Morris, coupled with his principles and exercises, became the foundation for the ministry of Skyhook. Here are logical steps you can take to have God's supernatural power guide you and lift you to your highest potential.

Here are some exercises to help you:

- Demote yourself to the top.
- Feed your five-thousand.
- Get rid of your biggest single expense.
- Have one-minute board meetings with the Chairman.
- Analyze your options and take the right fork in the road.
- Dig out clues for your future from events of your past.

This is a heavily packed, fast paced hour. People leave with simple steps to change their lives immediately. Many people brainstorm ideas from this program for months afterwards.

THE SUPERPOWER OF HUMILITY
(60-minute keynote)

The most difficult human attribute to attain is the very key that unlocks God's supernatural power to work in your life.

This program is a condensed study of chapters 12 and 13 of Paul's Letter to the Romans. It touches on the various ways Paul tells the members of the church how to act toward God, toward other believers, toward their enemies, and toward their government. The central theme Paul uses to teach these actions is humility. How does Paul's letter teach us how to act today? Most of us give only lip service to the word humility, but do we know:

- What real humility is?
- How do we create an attitude of humility?
- What are the obstacles to humility?
- When are we not humble?

This is a very thought provoking message that is designed to hit hard and make us look at ourselves, our lives, and our relationship with Christ.

You may contact Fred Morris at:

Skyhook
P.O. Box 344
Simpsonville, S.C.
29681

or

1-800-779-3619

or

www.skyhook.org

Part Four

Your Beginning Pages of Your Communication Journal

Your Beginning Pages of Your Communication Journal

In order to start your own communication journal, you might want to use the following form:

Key Word	Date	Text
Blessing	3/25/95	#600 Father, thank you for my Landlord reducing my rent by half, and putting me in be smaller building. It came at a time I desperately needed to cut my bills.
11/4/99 Question	11/4/99	Father, I am in a fog. I don't know which way to go. How can I build my ministry and work in my company too?

How to Sharpen Your Listening-to-God Skills

Key Word	Date	Text

Your Beginning Pages of Your Communication Journal

Key Word	Date	Text

How to Sharpen Your Listening-to-God Skills

Key Word	Date	Text

Your Beginning Pages of Your Communication Journal

Key Word	Date	Text

How to Sharpen Your Listening-to-God Skills

Key Word	Date	Text

Your Beginning Pages of Your Communication Journal

Key Word	Date	Text

How to Sharpen Your Listening-to-God Skills

Key Word	Date	Text

Your Beginning Pages of Your Communication Journal

Key Word	Date	Text

How to Sharpen Your Listening-to-God Skills

Key Word	Date	Text

Your Beginning Pages of Your Communication Journal

Key Word	Date	Text

How to Sharpen Your Listening-to-God Skills

Key Word	Date	Text

Your Beginning Pages of Your Communication Journal

Key Word	Date	Text

How to Sharpen Your Listening-to-God Skills

Key Word	Date	Text

Your Beginning Pages of Your Communication Journal

Key Word	Date	Text

How to Sharpen Your Listening-to-God Skills

Key Word	Date	Text

Your Beginning Pages of Your Communication Journal

Key Word	Date	Text

How to Sharpen Your Listening-to-God Skills

Key Word	Date	Text

Your Beginning Pages of Your Communication Journal

Key Word	Date	Text

How to Sharpen Your Listening-to-God Skills

Key Word	Date	Text

Your Beginning Pages of Your Communication Journal

Key Word	Date	Text

How to Sharpen Your Listening-to-God Skills

Key Word	Date	Text

Your Beginning Pages of Your Communication Journal

Key Word	Date	Text

Key Word	Date	Text

To order additional copies of

How to Sharpen Your Listening-to-God Skills

send $8.99* + $3.95 shipping and handling to:

WinePress Publishing
P.O. Box 1406
Mukilteo, WA 98275

Or have your credit card ready and call:

1-800-917-BOOK

*Quantity discounts avaliable